Visiting the Past

The Acropolis

Jane Shuter

Heinemann Library
Chicago, Illinois

© 2000 Reed Educational & Professional Publishing
Published by Heinemann Library,
an imprint of Reed Educational & Professional Publishing,
100 N. LaSalle, Suite 1010
Chicago, IL 60602

Customer Service 888-454-2279

Designed by Visual Image
Illustrations by David Cuzick and Visual Image
Printed in Hong Kong

04 03 02 01 00
10 9 8 7 6 5 4 3 2 1

Library of Congress Cataloging-in-Publication Data
Shuter, Jane.
 Acropolis / Jane Shuter.
  p. cm. – (Visiting the past)
 Includes bibliographical references and index.
 Summary: Discusses the history of the Acropolis, a large fortified
hill in the center of Athens, and the uses to which it and the
structures built upon it have been put throughout the ages.
 ISBN 1-57572-855-9
 1. Acropolis (Athens, Greece)—History Juvenile literature.
2. Athens (Greece)—Buildings, structures, etc. Pictorial works
Juvenile literature. 3. Historic monuments—Greece—Athens-
-Conservation and restoration Juvenile literature. [1. Acropolis
(Athens, Greece) 2. Athens (Greece)—Antiquities.] I. Title.
II. Series.
DF287.A2S54 1999
938'.5—dc21   99-14228
               CIP

Acknowledgments
The publishers would like to thank Richard Butcher and Magnet Harlequin for permission to reproduce all
photographs, except those on pages 14, 16, and 26, which are reproduced with permission of the Acropolis
Museum.

Cover photograph reproduced with permission of AKG London.

Some words are shown in bold, **like this.** You can find out what they mean by looking
in the glossary.

Contents

A Place of Safety 4

Classical Times 6

Destruction and Reconstruction 8

Ideas about the Gods 10

How Were Temples Used? 12

Ideas about War 14

Reflecting Real Life? 16

Beautiful Buildings 18

Builders at Work 20

Columns 22

Finishing Work 24

Statues and Carvings 26

Timeline 28

Glossary 30

More Books to Read 30

Index 32

A Place of Safety

Most Greek cities were built around an **acropolis**, which was a hilltop fortress or **citadel**. The most famous acropolis is in Athens. Called the Acropolis, it covers just over 10 acres (4 hectares), with a flat area on the top measuring 880 feet (268 meters) by 305 feet (93 meters). The Acropolis is famous for the **temples** and buildings that remain on it today, but it has been in use for thousands of years. The buildings were constantly repaired and replaced. They tell us a lot about how ancient Greek builders worked and give us an insight into ancient Greek ideas.

People began to use the Acropolis about 3000 B.C. It was used first as a safe place to live because it was high up and hard to reach. Its flat top was easy to build on, and it had freshwater springs, which meant that people did not have to keep hauling water up from the plains below. In about 1250 B.C., a king moved onto the Acropolis, making it a target for his enemies. The natural defense provided by the steep, rocky climb no longer gave enough protection. The king had strong stone walls built to **fortify** the sides of the Acropolis.

From the top of the Acropolis, people could see the countryside all around. The modern city of Athens covers most of that countryside now.

4

A place of worship

Hundreds of years passed and Athens grew. People moved down from the Acropolis to farm the plains around it. Greece developed into several **city-states**, including Athens, which often fought each other. The Athenians still used the Acropolis in times of danger, but its main use was as a place for worshiping the gods. The first temples were wooden, but about 675 B.C., the first stone temples were built, including one to the goddess after whom the city was named, Athena. In these buildings, as well as in the spaces between them, there were statues and places to make **offerings** to the various gods and goddesses.

Athens in peril

The Persians, who were old enemies of the Greek city-states, attacked Athens in 490 B.C., but were beaten by the heavily outnumbered Athenians at Marathon. The Athenians started a huge, new temple on the Acropolis to thank Athena for their victory. The Persians, meanwhile, plotted revenge. The new temple had barely risen above its stone **foundations** when, ten years later, the Persians were back, determined to conquer all of Greece. They burned Athens to the ground and destroyed everything on the Acropolis, but the Greeks drove the Persians off in a sea battle at Salamis.

The Athenians rebuilt their ruined city and repaired the Acropolis walls. Those Athenians who had fought the Persians decided not to repair their destroyed temples, but to leave them as a reminder of what had happened.

The ruins of the oldest stone temple to Athena are in the lower half of this photograph.

Classical Times

Many **city-states** felt that the Persians were still dangerous after the battle of Salamis, so they made an **alliance** called the Delian League. The Athenians, who had the biggest **fleet** of warships, were asked to lead it. Each city-state had to send ships to Athens to form part of a navy. However, most gave money instead, and Athens became richer and more powerful. Athens dominated the city-states of the League.

Athens made peace with Persia about 449 B.C. The Athenian leader, Pericles, wanted to rebuild the **temples** on the **Acropolis**—partly to please the gods and partly to show how rich and powerful Athens was. He called a meeting of all other city-states that had fought the Persians to discuss keeping the seas safe and whether to rebuild the temples. No one came because they resented Athens' growing power and did not want Pericles to order them about. Pericles had expected this and announced that the Athenians would decide for everyone. The Delian League had to continue paying Athens money for the navy, and the temples could be rebuilt.

Building the Parthenon

The Athenian Assembly met in 448 B.C. and approved the plans for the Parthenon. It was to be a grand new temple to replace the one begun more than 40 years before, after the Athenian victory at Marathon. By now there was even more to thank Athena for: the victory at Marathon, later victories over the Persians, and growing power over the other city-states. The Parthenon, and the statue of Athena inside it, would have to be very grand indeed to show enough gratitude.

Building work began in 448 B.C., and, despite interruptions, it was finished sixteen years later. The finished temple was as beautiful and awe-inspiring as Pericles had hoped, a wonderful **offering** to the goddess and an impressive display of the wealth and power of Athens.

The Parthenon, the big columned temple in the center of this artist's drawing, was the most magnificent building on the Acropolis.

Destruction and Reconstruction

For nearly a thousand years, the **Acropolis** remained almost untouched. When the Romans added Athens to their empire in 86 B.C., they did not destroy it, as the Persians had done, for they admired it, especially the Parthenon. Tourists came from all over the **Roman Empire.** They even bought copies of the huge statue of Athena in the Parthenon as souvenirs! The Romans kept the Greek **temples** repaired and added a few statues and a small circular **shrine** to Roman gods.

Athens remained part of the Roman Empire for hundreds of years. As the power of Rome declined, Athens had a number of different rulers before the Turks took over in about 1455. During this time, the temples of the Acropolis were used for Christian and, later, Muslim worship.

Turkish gunpowder

Because the Acropolis was the safest place for miles around, the Turks stacked the Propylaea—the buildings at the entrance—and the Parthenon with weapons and **gunpowder**. Unfortunately, nature and sailors from Venice, an old enemy of the Turks, both brought disaster. In 1656, lightning struck the gunpowder store in the Propylaea, blowing it apart. A later bombardment by the Venetians ignited more gunpowder, and the Parthenon, too, was blown apart. The Venetians took over Athens, temporarily.

The biggest change to the Acropolis in Roman times was the addition of a monument to the Roman general Agrippa to thank him for helping Athens when it was threatened by barbarians. This is the reconstructed base of that monument.

The Acropolis is constantly being repaired and **restored.** This is partly to repair damage done by the weather and bad pollution levels of Athens, and also to make the buildings more as they were before the explosions.

Most of the buildings on the Acropolis had been well preserved before 1687. By then, people thought the Acropolis's treasures were up for grabs. The Turks recaptured Athens but did not try to repair any of the damage. Many of the statues and carvings, even the smashed chunks of **marble**, were taken away. The marble was used as stone for building, to make lime for use in plaster, and as souvenirs. There had been twenty human statues and two horses on the western side of the Parthenon before 1687. By 1800, there were only four human statues left.

In 1801, the Turks gave the British **ambassador**, Lord Elgin, permission to take whatever he wanted from the Acropolis. Elgin, who was horrified by the way that the Acropolis was being **ransacked**, decided that the treasures of the Acropolis would be better off in British care. He shipped many carvings from the Parthenon back to England, where they can still be seen in the British Museum in London.

The Greeks eventually drove the Turks out of Athens in 1833. They began to restore the Acropolis. They pulled down all the buildings that had been added by the Turks and other invaders, and set about restoring and rebuilding the temples as accurately as they could. This work still continues today.

Workers try to use ancient Greek building techniques, but they also use modern technology, such as the metal scaffolding and crane in the picture. Visitors used to be able to walk around the temples of the Acropolis. Now the temples are roped off to stop people from climbing on them.

Ideas about the Gods

The ancient Greeks worshiped many different gods and goddesses. They thought of gods and goddesses as very like ordinary people—more beautiful, far more powerful, but driven by the same emotions. There is no holy book, like the Bible or the Koran, that tells us about their religion. But the ancient Greeks did have myths, or stories about the gods, that we can read or listen to today. The **Acropolis,** too, gives us clues about ancient Greek religion.

Athena versus Poseidon

Many ancient Greek cities had a god or goddess to take special care of their city. However, they did not ignore the other gods in case that would make them angry. According to myth, Athena, goddess of war and wisdom, and Poseidon, god of the sea, fought over who would be the special protector of Athens. The myth says Athena and Poseidon fought on the Acropolis. Poseidon stuck his **trident** into the ground and a salt-water spring erupted. Athena stuck her spear into the ground and an olive tree sprang up. Athena won. Some versions of the myth say that the chief god, Zeus, decided she had won, others say Athenians voted on it.

The first statue of Athena worshiped on the Acropolis was said to be carved from the wood of the olive tree she made spring from the ground. The Greeks did not think the statue was the goddess, but they did think that they had to treat it with as much care as if it were to show Athena how much they cared for her.

This olive tree stands where the first olive tree, said to have sprung from Athena's spear, stood. Some people say it is a shoot from the same roots.

The Acropolis and the city

The Acropolis tells us that the gods and goddesses the ancient Greeks worshiped were very important. The Athenians used the most visible, highest, best-defended place for their **temples**. They built their homes and public buildings around the Acropolis. The gods could watch over the city, and the citizens could look up from their daily lives and be reminded of the gods.

There were temples, **shrines,** and other places to worship in Athens itself, as well as on the Acropolis, but the Acropolis was the most important religious site. It was where all the big, public religious festivals took place and where the sacred statue of Athena was kept.

Even in modern Athens, with its tall buildings, the Acropolis still dominates the skyline.

The ancient Greeks built their temples to last. They were carefully made from expensive, heavy **marble**. Even the later explosions that ruined parts of the Acropolis did not destroy the buildings completely. The public buildings in Athens also were made from marble because they were important to the Athenians. The Athenians' own homes were made of sun-baked, mud bricks on stone **foundations**. Their walls were so soft and crumbled so easily that burglars were called wall piercers. The Greeks' homes were much less permanent than their temples.

The oldest buildings in Athens are in the area around the Acropolis. Even these date back only a few hundred years. None of the ordinary homes of ancient Athens have survived.

11

How Were Temples Used?

Ancient Greek **temples** were not like the churches, synagogues, or mosques of other religions. They were not places that people went into to worship. They were, instead, places where statues and other **artifacts** of the gods or goddesses of the temple were placed and cared for by priests or priestesses. They were, in a way, homes for the gods. The ancient Greeks did not believe that the gods really lived in these temples, but they believed that acting as if they did, showed the gods respect. Temples were designed to be beautiful. The gods were believed to enjoy looking at beautiful buildings and statues.

The ancient Greeks did worship at the temples, but they worshiped outside. Religious ceremonies always included prayers and **sacrifices** at altars, often to the east of the temple. Temples were designed so that the statue of the god could look out the end of the temple toward the altar and witness the sacrifice.

The gods could look out the doorways of temples, from the inner room, to the sacrifices taking place outside.

If people could not go into the temples, how did they worship their gods? There were many different ways to worship. People could say a quiet prayer to a particular god or goddess by a statue or **shrine**. They could leave something they valued as an **offering**. What they left depended on how rich the givers were and what they wanted from the gods. Offerings did not have to be expensive to please the gods, but they had to mean a lot to the giver. A string of cheap beads given to a woman by someone she loved, for example, would be valuable to the giver.

Religious festivals

The big religious festivals were held on the **Acropolis**. People marched up to the Acropolis along the Panathenic Way, the main path to the Acropolis from the city, to pray outside the temple and watch the sacrifices. They ate the meat of the animals that were sacrificed as part of the ceremony.

Big festivals, which lasted several days, were not just sacrifices and prayers. There were musical performances and plays performed at the theaters. There were sporting events, such as races, wrestling, and throwing competitions. These things were not done just for fun but as offerings to the gods.

This rough path was the most direct route to the Acropolis from the **agora**, the main square of Athens. There were other routes, including the Panathenic Way, used during the yearly festival for Athena.

The theater of Dionysus, god of wine, lies just below the walls of the Acropolis. Plays were performed for religious festivals.

Ideas about War

Greek **city-states** were small and did not have full-time armies. They expected all men to fight when the city-state was threatened either by other city-states or by foreign enemies, like the Persians. Most Greek men would fight for their city-state at least once in their lives. Ancient Greek stories were full of battles and heroic deeds. Men were expected to fight bravely and, if they died defending their city state, they were honored.

The **Acropolis** tells us about the ancient Greeks and war in several ways. The fact that the city-state grew up around the Acropolis, which is basically a defensive site, tells us that the Greeks were always poised for war, trying to guard against attack. Also, the goddess they chose as the special protector of the city and worshiped on the Acropolis, was a warrior goddess. Athena was worshiped in several different ways in ancient Greece. She was the goddess of wisdom, but she was also the goddess of war and of victory, as Athena Nike. She was shown with a helmet, spear, and shield to emphasize this fact.

The Athenians thought that Athena's warlike nature would be good for the city she guarded and would bring them victory.

Honoring the brave

The Acropolis also tells us that the Athenians believed in honoring the men who died fighting for it. Athena did not always bring victory. Sometimes even the buildings on the Acropolis were destroyed. But, to the Athenians, victories and defeats had to be remembered, and those who fought and died were to be honored.

When the Persians took Athens in 480 B.C., stone from the destroyed **temples** on the Acropolis was used to repair its walls. Stones from the **columns** of the temple to Athena were set into the repaired walls where they could be seen from the **agora**, or main square. The use of these stones was both an early war memorial and a warning to the people of the city to be on their guard.

The Athenians also celebrated victories. Decorative carvings on the Parthenon show one of the festivals to Athena held every four years, the Great Panathenaia. Historians think that the carvings show the last Panathenaia before the great battle of Marathon against the Persians in 490 B.C. It celebrates the victory at Marathon, which the Greeks believed Athena helped them win. It also remembers the men who died there.

The reused columns from behind, inside the Acropolis. If you look closely, you can just see the decorated edge on the column marked.

From the agora, the columns reused as a memorial show on the left side of the temple on the Acropolis.

Reflecting Real Life?

The **Acropolis** tells us of Greek ideas about the gods and war. It also tells us, as we shall see, a lot about ancient Greek building methods. Does it tell us anything about the people themselves, or their everyday lives? In some ways, it cannot do this. During much of its existence, the Acropolis was not a place where people lived or even visited daily. But there are some things we can find out.

The carvings, especially those on the Parthenon, show what people looked like, how they dressed and styled their hair. They also show some furniture, jars, and boxes. Most of these carvings are no longer on the Parthenon, nor even in the museum on the Acropolis. Those that have not been destroyed have been scattered across the world. A large collection of carvings, called the Elgin Marbles, is in the British Museum in London, England. However, the Acropolis Museum has **artifacts** from several time periods, which give interesting information.

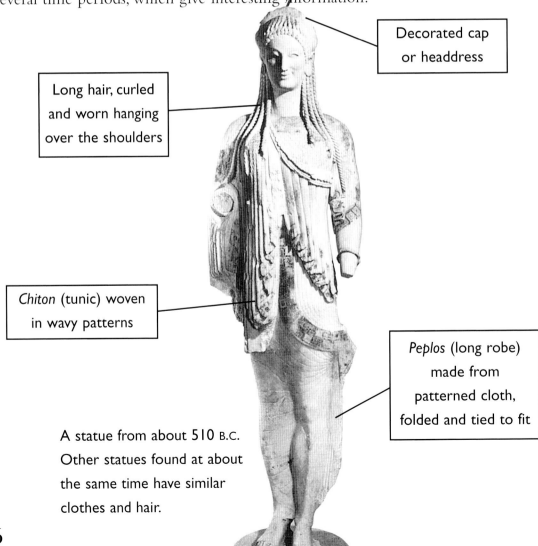

Decorated cap or headdress

Long hair, curled and worn hanging over the shoulders

Chiton (tunic) woven in wavy patterns

Peplos (long robe) made from patterned cloth, folded and tied to fit

A statue from about 510 B.C. Other statues found at about the same time have similar clothes and hair.

Athenian clothing

In some ways, the women shown are dressed very similarly, considering that the statues were made a century apart. They look much more alike than a woman from 1899 and one from 1999 would. They have long, loose clothing with lots of drapes and folds. Their hair is long and worn in complicated styles. There are changes in the way the clothes are fastened and the way the hair is fixed, but the general style was best for the climate, so no one saw the need to change the design.

Men wore similar clothes. In poorer families, men and women of similar size often shared clothing. The differences in clothes had more to do with wealth than gender. Poorer men and women, who needed to work in their clothes, wore shorter, simpler tunics. The rich wore the longer, more draped styles.

Long hair, styled in ringlets

Long robe, loosely draped, tied at the waist and fastened at the shoulders. It was not tied up in the same way as the earlier *peplos*.

The cloth could have been patterned. The decoration is long gone from the original statues.

This is an exact copy of one of the female statues supporting a porch of the Erechtheum **temple** of Acropolis. The originals, which were made in about B.C., were either stolen or badly damaged by air pollution. Other statues found at about the same time have similar clothes and hair.

Beautiful Buildings

The ancient Greeks had a very mathematical view of architecture. They thought that the most beautiful buildings were those that were **symmetrical** and in **proportion**. Every measurement had to balance and work in relation to every other measurement. Only then would the building look right. This applied to all buildings—theaters and public buildings, as well as **temples**.

A perfect example of this is the Parthenon, the biggest and most important temple on the **Acropolis**. Pericles wanted it to be the most beautiful and perfect temple ever built. The proportions of the Parthenon, shown in the picture below, were designed very carefully so that everything worked out at a **ratio** of nine to four. The measurements marked on the photo show what this means. The length and width of the temple also fitted this ratio, although we cannot see them on this photo.

This photo of the Parthenon shows how the ancient Greeks' use of ratios worked in practice. The height of the **columns** (A) is four-ninths the width of the Parthenon (B). The width of each column (C) is four-ninths the distance between them (D).

Building in style

Proportion was important, but this does not mean that everything on an ancient Greek building measured exactly straight. They had to *look* elegant and in proportion, and sometimes this meant using little tricks in the building.

The floor of the Parthenon rises very slightly in the center, and the columns get narrower toward the top, seemingly in a smooth line. To create this effect, the builders had to make a bulge in the columns about two-thirds of the way up. Also, the columns do not go straight up, they tilt inward slightly. All these changes mean that the building does not look like a square-sided box. It looks elegant and in proportion.

The square sides of the photograph help show how the column angles tilt. The changes in floor level and column width are probably too small to notice in a photo.

Architects thought that temples needed to be raised, so they could be seen, but not so high that they could not be looked at comfortably. Almost all temples have three marble steps, which are set on top of low foundations of ordinary stone.

19

Builders at Work

Ancient Greek builders paid just as much attention to detail as architects did. They thought it was important that the visitor's gaze flowed smoothly over a beautiful building. They made sure that each brick or section of a **column** fitted together so that the finished wall or column looked as if it were made from a single piece of **marble**. They wanted the joints to be as invisible as possible. Despite having only a few simple iron tools and very basic lifting equipment, they still managed to accomplish their goals.

Builders took great care over the visible parts of their buildings. Parts that were not going to be seen, however, did not have to be beautiful. They just had to work. When it was decided that the Parthenon would be bigger than originally planned, the builders extended the **foundations** using whatever stone came to hand to make a flat surface. They did not bother to match up the size of the stone with the old foundations. The foundations were not meant to be seen.

The ground level on the Acropolis is lower now than it was when the **temples** were built, mainly because of damage and **erosion.** It is now possible to see the foundations of the Parthenon and how they were extended.

The clamps that held the marble or stone blocks together were on the inside, and could not be seen on the finished building. However, several buildings on the **Acropolis** were damaged, and we can see how the builders worked by examining pieces of marble that are no longer part of the building.

This iron clamp, used in a modern piece of restoration, was not covered in lead. It has started to rust.

This block was joined to the next one by an iron clamp that fitted into this T-shaped hole. The ancient Greek builders covered each clamp in lead, which kept the water out and stopped the iron from rusting.

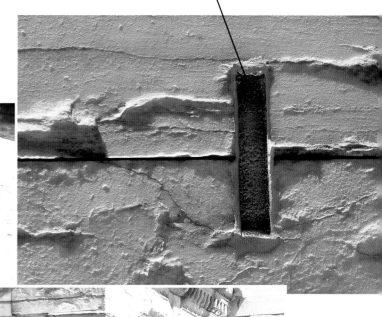

This piece of marble was deliberately roughened so that the piece that went over it could grip it tightly.

The wall to the right is damaged, so the joints are more evident, but after thousands of years, the blocks still fit together tightly.

Columns

The ancient Greeks used two styles of **columns** to hold up their buildings, **Doric** columns and **Ionic** columns. There are examples of both on the **Acropolis**, used deliberately to contrast with each other. So the Parthenon, designed to be a substantial, imposing building, has Doric columns. The smaller Erechtheum temple nearby has Ionic columns; it made a deliberate contrast with the Parthenon. The Propylaea at the entrance used both styles of columns.

Ionic columns (shown below) were slimmer and more ornate than Doric columns. They had a decorated base and **capital**. This style was particularly associated with Athens and eastern Greece.

Doric columns (shown above) sit directly on the floor of the **temple** and have a plain capital at the top.

This column has been rebuilt as carefully as possible, but the damage done over time means that you can see that it is made up of several different drums. The picture below shows the way the columns would have joined together tightly and evenly.

The column sections, or drums, were cut into shape at the **quarry**. The handles at the side are for ropes slung around it to lift it into place. These lifting handles were chipped off once the column was in place. Each drum was fixed to the one below it by a fixing pin in a hole through the middle.

This is a drum from the bottom of a column. The face showing would have sat directly on the floor of the temple. We know this, because it has no hole for the pin to secure it to the next drum down. Also, the edges have been **fluted**, or shaped into vertical grooves. Fluting was done after the drums were in place. The bottom drum, however, was done ahead of time so that the fluting ran all the way to the floor.

Finishing Work

Once all the parts of the **temple** were in place, it was time for the finishing work. Before the decorative carvings and the statues were put in place, craftsmen had to **flute** the **columns**, decorate the tops and bottoms of the columns, and tile the roof. They also had to do any carving around doorways or on ceilings.

Fluting was time consuming and took a great deal of skill. It did not make the columns any stronger, but it did make them more beautiful. And, of course, the gods, knowing how hard it was to do and how long it took, would appreciate the skill that went into it.

Doric and **Ionic** columns had different kinds of fluting, both done after the column drums had been fitted together, so that each flute made one smooth sweep down the column. Doric columns have 20 flutes, which touch each other at a sharp edge. Ionic columns, though narrower, have more flutes—24 of them, separated from each other by a smooth band.

The ceiling of the Erechtheion is carved. There is also decorative carving on the wall and over the door.

The base of this Ionic column of the Erechtheum has been decorated. You can also see the flutes and the flattened band that separates them.

24

Roofing the Parthenon

The roofs of almost all ancient Greek houses, public buildings, and temples were made from **terra-cotta**, shaped in molds and left to dry in the sun. The roof of the Parthenon, however, was covered with **marble** tiles, so that even the roof shone in the sun. Although marble tiles were made to the same design and fixed to the roof in the same way as terra-cotta tiles, they gave the builders special problems.

Marble was far heavier than terra-cotta and much more difficult to use in making roof tiles. The tiles could not be too thick, or they would be so heavy that the structure would not be able to take the weight. They could not be made too thin or wide either, or they would crack too easily. They might even split while they were being made, so they had to be made fairly small.

The wider tiles were put on the wooden roof frame, with their curved edges facing upward.

Smaller V-shaped tiles were then put on top, to hold the edges of the bottom tiles together.

The **restorers** have found some marble roof tiles and put them together to show visitors to the Acropolis how they worked. Many of the older buildings in Athens are roofed in terra-cotta tiles using the same system.

These decorated end-pieces stood along the end of the roof, to help hold the tiles in place.

Statues and Carvings

The buildings and scattered pieces of **marble** on the **Acropolis** can give us a good idea about the building process. They tell us less about what the finished buildings would have looked like when filled with statues and covered with carvings, which were all beautifully painted and decorated with gold. While the skill of Greek builders and **sculptors** is admired, we know very little about the skill of their painters. Many people, in fact, do not even realize that many statues and buildings were once painted.

There are two main reasons for this. First, over thousands of years, weather, environmental pollution, and general wear and tear have worn away much of the color from the marble that is left. Second, there are only a few original statues and carvings on the site. These are in the museum, where they are kept safe from further attacks by the weather and pollution. Many of the statues and carvings have been taken away to museums and other places all over the world, and even these have largely lost their color. So when you next look at a Greek statue, or a picture of one, try to imagine what it would have looked like when it was beautifully painted.

From earliest times, the carvings on the Acropolis were painted to make them more colorful. These figures were on the eastern side of the Parthenon.

We do know that a huge number of sculptors worked on the site, carving all the decorative carvings. Some of them were better than others. All of them could, of course, carve figures that looked like people and horses, but some of these figures were incredibly lifelike.

Unlike most sculptures that decorate buildings, the ones on the Parthenon were carved as if they were statues, not flat at the back. The details on the backs of the carvings are just as carefully done as the fronts, despite the fact that, in most cases, they would never be seen. This is another example of the desire to make this building absolutely perfect, reflecting both the glory of the city-state of Athens and its people's gratitude to their protector Athena.

This carving on the right is part of a series on the Parthenon, showing a **mythological** battle between centaurs—or half-man, half-horse—and humans. It was made by one of the best sculptors, and looks very lifelike and full of movement.

The other carving still in place on the Parthenon is over the front porch. It is part of the myth of the birth of Athena.

Timeline

c.3000 B.C.   First settlement established on the **Acropolis.**

1250 B.C.   Palace built on the Acropolis for Mycenaean king. Walls are built to strengthen the natural defenses of the hill.

675 B.C.   First stone **temples** built on the Acropolis.

490 B.C.   Persian invasion of Greece defeated at the battle of Marathon.

480 B.C.   Persian invasion of Greece defeated at the battle of Salamis.

449 B.C.   Athenians make peace with Persia.

448 B.C.   Plans approved for building the Parthenon.

447 B.C.   Parthenon begun.

432 B.C.   Parthenon finished.

86 B.C.   Athens becomes part of the **Roman Empire.**

A.D. 269   Romans driven out of Athens. The invading barbarians, called Goths, take over for a while. Various tribes then control the city. These include Christians, who use the Acropolis as a fort and build a Christian church inside the Parthenon.

1455   Turks take over Athens.

1656   Propylaea damaged by **gunpowder** explosion, set off by lightning.

1687   Parthenon damaged by explosion caused by gunpowder set off by Venetian attack.

1801   Turks allow Lord Elgin to remove the sculptures from the Parthenon. Known as the Elgin Marbles, they are now in the British Museum.

1833   Athens comes under Greek control.

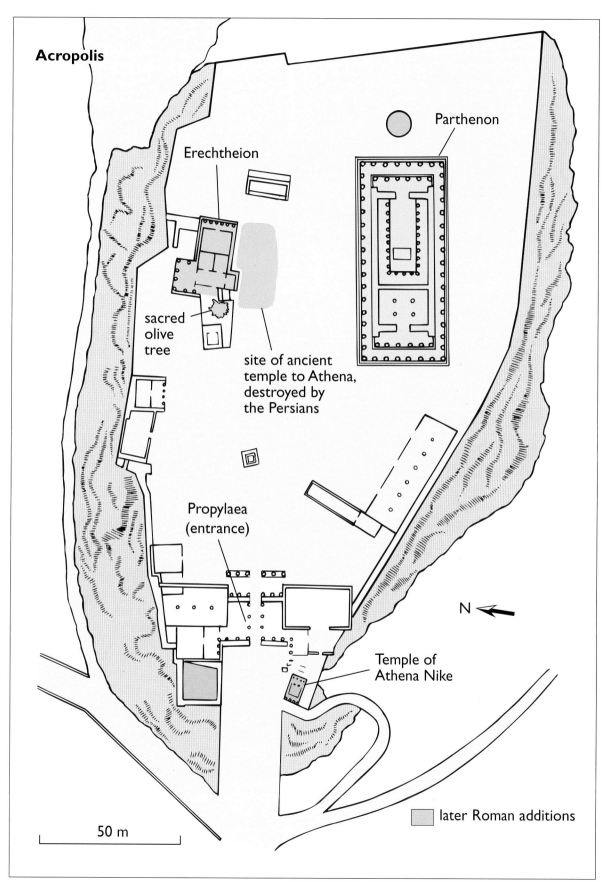

Acropolis

Erechtheion

Parthenon

sacred
olive
tree

site of ancient
temple to Athena,
destroyed by
the Persians

Propylaea
(entrance)

N

Temple of
Athena Nike

50 m

later Roman additions

29

Glossary

acropolis hilltop fortress in ancient Greece, the Acropolis in Athens being the most famous.

agora main square of a city in ancient Greece

alliance agreement among different people or groups of people to work together for a common goal

ambassador person who goes to another country to act as a representative for his or her own country

artifact something made by humans, often of a historical or religious significance

capital head, or top, of a pillar or column

citadel fortified center of a town or city

city-state independent state made up of a city and the countryside around it

column cylinder-shaped support for the roof of a building

Doric simple style of column or other architecture, named for an ancient people called the Dorians

erosion process of being worn away over time, often by the weather

fortify to strengthen, or to add defensive walls or weapons

fleet group of ships under the control of one commander

fluting decorative grooves that run from top to bottom on a column

foundation stone base for a building

gunpowder mixture of saltpeter, charcoal, and sulfur that explodes when lit

Ionic style of column or other architecture with many decorations, especially ornate capitals, named for the people of the Greek Ionian islands

marble very hard kind of limestone, which can be polished to become shiny and smooth

mythological according to a traditional myth or story

offering something given to the gods as a show of respect or gratitude

quarry place where stone is dug out of the ground, usually to be used for building work

proportion harmony or balance in the shape of something

ransack to search thoroughly or violently, especially when robbing a building

ratio way of multiplying groups of numbers so that they all fit the same pattern

restore to put something that has been changed back into its original form

Roman Empire area conquered by the Roman armies, beginning in about 510 B.C., circling the Mediterranean Sea and stretching from Britain in the north to Egypt in the south

sacrifice to kill an animal or person as an offering to the gods

sculptor person who carves stone into statues or decorations on buildings

shrine special place dedicated to a god or goddess, not as grand as a temple

symmetry exact match between the opposite halves of a figure or building

temple religious building built to honor a god or goddess

terra-cotta hard reddish-brown clay that is baked hard and then used in building

trident spear with three prongs, like a fork

More Books to Read

MacDonald, Fiona and Mark Bergin. *A Greek Temple.* Lincolnwood, Ill: NTC Contemporary Publishing Company, 1992.

Nardo, Don. *The Parthenon of Ancient Greece.* San Diego: Lucent Books. 1999.

Shuter, Jane. *Builders, Craftsmen & Traders.* Des Plaines, Ill: Heinemann Library, 1998.

Vernerey, Denise. Translated by Mary K. LaRose. *The Ancient Greeks: In the Land of the Gods.* Brookfield, Conn: Millbrook Press, 1996.

Index

agora 13
Agrippa 8
Athena 5, 6, 10, 13, 14, 15, 26
Athens 4, 5, 6, 11, 14, 28

carvings 9, 16, 24, 26, 27
clothing 16, 17
columns 15, 19, 20, 22, 23, 24

Delian League 6
Doric columns 22, 24

Elgin, Lord 9, 16, 28
Erechtheum 17, 22, 24

foundations 5, 20

gods and goddesses 5, 10, 11
Great Panathenaia 6, 15
gunpowder 8, 28

hair 16, 17

Ionic columns 22, 24

marble 9, 11
Marathon, battle of 5, 6, 15, 28

offerings 5, 6, 13,

Panathenic Way 13
Parthenon 6, 8, 9, 15, 16, 18, 19,
    20, 22, 25, 26, 27, 28
Pericles 6, 18
Persians 5, 6, 14, 15, 28
Poseidon 10
Propylaea 8, 22

ratios 18
religion 10, 12, 13
Romans 8, 28

sacrifices 12
Salamis, battle of 5, 6, 28
sculpture 26, 27
statues 5, 9, 10, 11, 12, 16, 17, 24,
    26, 27

temples 4, 6, 11, 12, 19,
terra-cotta 25
Turks 8, 9, 28

Venetians 8, 28

Zeus 10